I Once Was Lost

One Woman's Exodus From the
Depths of the Church

I Once Was Lost: One Woman's Exodus from the Depths of the Church
Copyright © 2025 by Shannon Nuszen
All rights reserved.

This book, or any portion of it, may not be reproduced or transmitted electronically, mechanically, or by any other means including but not limited to photocopying, scanning, downloading, etc., without prior written permission of the author.

For sales inquiries, contact: info@beyneynu.com

Cover illustration by Monique Letourneau.
Cover and interior design by the Virtual Paintbrush.

ISBN 979-8-9926463-0-6 (hardcover)
ISBN 979-8-9926463-1-3 (paperback)

First Edition 2025

www.beyneynu.com

I Once Was Lost

One Woman's Exodus From the Depths of the Church

SHANNON NUSZEN

Cover Art

THE COVER ART, created by Monique Letourneau—a dedicated volunteer for Beyneynu, a *Bat Noach*, beautifully captures the heart of this journey.

It depicts Shannon's courageous steps out of the church, leaving behind the safe and familiar world she had always known. Facing the vast and uncertain desert beyond, she discovers she is not alone. To her amazement, she finds herself among thousands—perhaps even hundreds of thousands—who are walking the same path.

This mass exodus, foretold in the Tanach, reflects a prophetic movement as we draw closer to Redemption, with people from all walks of life coming to know the one true God of Israel. Monique's artwork eloquently conveys the bravery, hope, and connection that define this transformative journey.

Dedication

לאמי היהודייה האהובה,

פרידה נוסן ז״ל,

שהיית לי כאם והייתה אור מדריך בהחדרת
ערכים יהודיים לחיים בתוך בית חם ואוהב.
אני מתגעגע אלייך מאוד, אמא.

ולעילוי נשמת אחייני היקר,

בנימין איירלי ז״ל,

אשר מסר את חייו בעזה בהגנה על הארץ שאהב,
לאחר הזוועות של ה-7 באוקטובר 2023.

ולעילוי נשמת

הרב ישראל רוזן ז״ל,

שללא עזרתו לא היינו מגיעים למקום
שבו אנו נמצאים היום.

ZAMIR COHEN	זמיר כהן
Rosh Yeshivah Of "Heichal Meir"	ישיבת "היכל מאיר"
Rabbi of the Etrog neighborhood	רבנות אתרוג ביתר עלית
Author Responsa "Nezer Cohen" book	שו"ת 'נזר כהן' ועוד
Hatam Sofer St. 5 Betar Eilit	חתם סופר 5 ביתר עלית

בס"ד, ג' אדר תשפ"ג

מכתב ברכה

הנני בזה בשבח ארגון 'ביננו' העוסק בין היתר באיתור וחשיפת מיסיונרים נוצרים המתחפשים ליהודים, נטמעים בקהילות יהודיות-חרדיות וזורעים הרס וחורבן בכרם ישראל מבפנים ר"ל.

בשנים האחרונות המיסיון הנוצרי הרחיב את מטרותיו ושיפר את דרכי פעולתו, ולמרבה הזעזוע והתדהמה יש מהמיסיונרים המרכזים את מאמציהם בניסיונות לחדור בעורמה לקהילות יהודיות באמצעות התחזות ליהודים ואפילו לרבנים ותחת מסכה זו עורכים חתונות, כותבים סת"מ ואף עורכים גיורים וכותבים גיטין לזוגות נשואים. אין צורך להאריך בהשלכות ההלכתיות אשר לעיתים הינן בלתי הפיכות ר"ל.

הנה שמעתי המלצות נאמנות על ארגון 'ביננו' ובראשות הגב' שאנון נוסן שיחי' אשר פועלים רבות לחשיפת המיסיונרים הללו הבאים בדרכי רמייה, באמצעות סילוק המסכה שעל פניהם והתרעה בשער בת רבים, מביאים לצמצום משמעותי ואף להפסקת פעילותם הנלוזה. ואף גם זאת פועלים הם למניעת כניסת מיסיונרים לארץ הקודש על ידי השתדלות מול הרשויות והגורמים המתאימים.

לא נצרכא אלא לברכה שחפץ ה' בידם יצלח ויוסיפו בעבודת הקודש להגנה על כרם בית ה' מהמיסיון הנוצרי, ומה' ישאו ברכה על כל עמלם.

הכו"ח בברכה נאמנה

Table of Contents

About the Author 9
Acknowledgements 11
Important Warning. 14
Introduction 16
A Presence Always Near. 19
The Gospel Stories I Grew Up On. 20
Was He Really There?. 22
You Say YouLove Me? 24
Faith the Size of a Mustard Seed 26
Who Left Who?. 28
A Holy Home. 30
To the Jew First 32
The Truth I Knew. 34
To Serve and to Share. 36
A Careful Cross 38
The Language of Love 40
The Fascination of Faith 42
The Mission to Reach 44
A Vessel for Your Will 46
Come Wrestle with Me 48
Let's Get Biblical 50
The Silent Struggle 52
The Silent Departure. 54
When Love Turns to Hate .56

Shattered and Free 59
An Exodus. 62
Homecoming. 64
How Long Can This Last? 68
A Friday Night I'll Never Forget 70
The Elephant in the Room 73
Dizzy with Discovery 75
What Have I Done? 78
The Three Times 80
Knocking Again 82
Determined to Grow. 84
The Beit Din 86
Longing to Belong 88
Flaws and All 90
Thank You 92
Don't Touch the Wine 94
Limbo Ends 96
Giants of Torah. 98
Rabbi Yisrael Rozen 100
The Mikvah. 103
A New Life, A New Family 104
Under the Chuppah in Hebron 107
A Wound, A Gift 108
A New Chapter in the Promised Land. 111
Pinch Me. 112
But Now I'm Found 114
And Then What? 116
Reviews/Recommendations. 123

About the Author

SHANNON NUSZEN, a former Evangelical Christian missionary, was raised in the world of Christian scriptural polemics as the daughter of a minister. Once deeply involved in the Christian messianic movement, she later converted to Judaism and has since dedicated her life to exposing missionary tactics targeting Jews. Drawing from her firsthand experience, she educates Jewish communities worldwide on the dangers of deceptive proselytization. Shannon is the founder of Beyneynu, an organization that monitors missionary activity worldwide and advocates for proper boundaries and guidelines with faith-based organizations. Her story has been featured in *The Jerusalem Post*, Aish HaTorah, *Ami Magazine*, *Mishpacha*, the Orthodox Union, and other major publications.

Acknowledgements

TO EVERYONE WHO encouraged me on this journey, I offer my deepest gratitude. If you welcomed me at your *Shabbat* or *Chag* table, thank you for your warmth and hospitality.

A special thank you to those who defended me, stood up for me, wrote recommendations to the *beit din*, reached out when I was struggling, or went out of their way to support me at any point along this path. There are too many of you to name, but your kindness and courage will never be forgotten.

To my mother and father Neil Hines and Michal Picquet. I know this journey has changed our family a lot, and I appreciate that you've rolled with it.

To my children, Samantha and Reuven, thank you for enduring the hard times and celebrating the good ones. This wasn't just my journey; it was yours as well. I am so proud of the incredible individuals you have become. To my daughters, Daphna and Zipporah, thank you for your patience and for your unwavering commitment to making our house a home. I am honored to be your Ima.

To my husband, Jack: Thank you for your unwavering love and support, for always taking care of me, and for your tireless dedication and hard work. Your efforts have given our family the opportunity to build a life here and have allowed our children to fully embrace and acclimate to Israeli life—a dream we once thought impossible.

Thank you to Michael and Susan Abramowitz, who took me under their wing and became like second parents to me throughout this journey. To Avi and Ruti Eastman—Coach and DaMomma—thank you for being my family in Israel and my ride-or-die companions. Your support and love have meant the world to me.

Thank you to the staff of Jewish Israel, and friends Avraham and Shulamit Leibler, Ellen Horowitz, Anita Tucker, Judy Lash-Balint. To Rabbi Stuart Federow and Sam Shube, who encouraged me to speak out when I preferred to stay behind the scenes.

To Jonathan Sacerdoti, whose keen investigative eye and unwavering Jewish spirit inspired him to pursue one shocking case after another. His unparalleled professionalism stands out among journalists, and he has taught me more than he likely realizes.

To the one family from the church who never turned their back on me—Steve and Debbie Majors, Paul, Kevin, and Stacey—thank you for your steadfast love. You understand the path I've chosen and the work I do, yet you choose to embrace me without judgment, leaving the rest in God's hands.

To Rabbi Yisrael Rozen, *z"l*, who moved mountains for my family and me, and to Rabbis Shmuel Eliyahu, Dov Lior, Raffi Ostroff, and Dan Marans, I owe an eternal debt of gratitude. Without your backbone, guidance, and support, we would not be where we are today.

Thank you to all my *Bnei Noach* friends, the TanakTalk

community, Beyneynu volunteers, and supporters from around the world. I can't name the thousands of you here, but you know who you are, and I'm deeply grateful.

Lastly, to Rabbi Tovia Singer, whose work turned my world upside down and changed it forever: Thank you for your unwavering dedication and compassion. You have profoundly impacted not only my life but also the lives of my children, my father, and countless others who have chosen this path. Your efforts have sparked a monumental shift, leading to a mass exodus from the church and, please God, toward the final Redemption.

Thank you all for being part of this incredible journey.

Important Warning

*B*EFORE YOU BEGIN reading these pages, it's deeply important that you read the Introduction in order to understand the mindset they were written in and the experience that it's meant to bring you through. Without this understanding the content may be difficult to understand and even offensive if you don't understand their purpose and the experience that's meant to bring you through.

Readers will notice that some lines of the narrative poetry, particularly in the first half of the book, are footnoted. Nearly all these references come from the Christian Bible, specifically the New Testament. These citations highlight the theological background of certain poetic phrases, illustrating how deeply embedded New Testament doctrines were in my beliefs and practices.

For Christian readers, encountering these doctrines through a different lens can sometimes provoke discomfort, often met with hostility or denial. The footnotes are there to guide readers to the original theological sources, encouraging them to examine these doctrines for themselves. One of the most important lessons I learned on this journey was to never take someone's word for it—always look it up and study it for yourself.

That said, I am not suggesting that Jewish readers seek out these citations. Understanding them fully requires a level of familiarity with Christian theology that, for most Jews, may not be particularly useful—except for those dedicated to helping others transition out of the church. However, even without this context, the book remains valuable as a psycho-emotional map of my transition from one world to another.

Introduction

I'VE READ MANY books about people's journeys out of the church—some of them I highly recommend. But when it came time to write my own, I realized there were things I couldn't bring myself to say. There is trauma and a depth of experience that I am simply not ready to put into words.

This book is not a reflective explanation of how I arrived here. It is not written to unravel the past or offer a step-by-step account of my journey. Instead, it's an immersive experience—a way to walk through it with me. Because of this, I feel compelled to include a trigger warning: this book is raw and unfiltered in its delivery.

My purpose is to let you feel what it was like. For those who have shared a similar path, this book may bring back vivid memories and feelings you've perhaps forgotten. But for others—especially those who have never experienced life in the church or been raised the way I was—I hope this provides a window into the missionary mindset.

Through these pages, I want you to understand the connection, the desire to please, the fear of disobedience or doubting one's faith, and the internal tug-of-war that defined each step of my journey. Only by walking in another's shoes, by truly feeling and understanding their perspective, can we foster genuine compassion.

When I speak publicly, I often address Jewish audiences about the dangers of missionary efforts aimed at converting Jews. My goal is not just to warn but also to encourage compassion and understanding for the people involved. This isn't an easy balance to strike, and I understand that it may be controversial. The mission to convert is harmful and deeply hurtful to Jews—but the messenger often acts out of ignorance, unaware of the betrayal they would feel if they encountered the truth.

It is my hope that Jewish readers will come away from this book with a clearer understanding of why Christian missionary efforts pose a threat to our people, and why there is such an intense need for boundaries and guidelines in interfaith relationships. At the same time, I hope to inspire greater empathy and acceptance for those who break free from that world—those who approach Judaism with sincere, open hearts, often at great personal cost. Many leave behind shattered families, broken relationships, and the only community they've ever known.

The Torah refers to a convert as an orphan, emphasizing the Jewish community's responsibility to welcome them as family. To wound a convert, to compound their pain, is a serious transgression. The Torah teaches that it is God Himself who watches over the convert and intervenes on their behalf.

May this book not only serve as a warning, but also as a reminder of the profound care and compassion we are called to show to those who seek to join our people, even amidst their own brokenness.

A Presence Always Near

From my cradle, I knew He was there,
A presence that lingered everywhere.
He knew my thoughts, my every care,
And I could swear I felt Him near.

Through my days, I'd softly speak,
In Him, I found the love I'd seek.
A silent friend, my soul's embrace,
His warmth, His light, a sacred space.

He knew me like none ever could,
Loved me when none other would.
In my shadows, He was my guide,
Through every sorrow, by my side.

Jesus, a part of me so true,
A love eternal, forever new.[1]
No matter the paths my life may choose,
I was sure that Him, I'd never lose.[2]

---

1 Hebrews 13:8
2 Matthew 28:20

The Gospel Stories I Grew Up On

THE GOSPEL STORIES I grew up on became my truth,
Jesus loved me, I was told, since my youth.
So much love, He gave his life for me,[1]
A mystery too vast for a child of three.

What sin had I done to put Him there?
A burden of death my small heart couldn't bear.
But I bore it still, heavy and grim,
Shaping my world, all to please Him.

Constant guilt and a soul laid bare,
Humiliation wrapped in whispered prayer.
I longed to make Him proud, to be free,
Yet the sin of my being loomed heavily.

What sin could weigh so much, I asked in fear?
"There's no measure," they said, "it's all severe."[2]
A midnight snack or a secret untold,
Each as dark as the crimes of the bold.[3]

---

1 John 3:16
2 James 2:10
3 Romans 3:23

"Odd," you say, "how can this be?"
But it's in His word, and His word is decree.
To question is folly, to doubt is sin,
So I buried my thoughts, deep within.

Yet whispers lingered, soft and defied—
Could love be so cruel? Or had they lied?
The gospel stories I grew up on became my truth,
But truth, I've learned, can evolve from youth.

Was He Really There?

Jesus was with me every step of the way,
Through trials and tribulations, come what may.[1]
I cried to Him when my parents fought,
When love was scarce and me they forgot.

When the nights brought a predator to my bed,
Was He there then? Watching instead?
I told Him of it, my whispered plea,
And of the next one, and their cruelty.

When I grew older, that elder's touch
Alone in that room, he took too much —
He was there, or so I believed,
Listening to the confusion I grieved.

Through it all, Jesus, my constant friend,[2]
A solace I clung to, a hope without end.
Without Him, I don't know what I'd have done,
But was He really there—or was it just me?

---

1   Hebrews 13:5
2   John 15:15

Was it my strength, my own unseen fight,
That carried me forward through each dark night?
Perhaps He was there, or perhaps only me,
Bearing the burden no one else could see.

You Say You Love Me?

Like *"a thief in the night,"*[1] they said you'd come,
For those who believe, the faithful ones.
In the *"twinkling of an eye,"*[2] the saved would ascend,
And the rest, abandoned, to a dark, bitter end.

The *tribulation*—a time of despair,
When Satan's rule would poison the air.
The *Antichrist*'s mark, a deadly decree,
Refuse it—Then hell is where you'll be.

To miss the Rapture, to be "left behind,"[3]
Was the terror that haunted my young mind.
A guillotine waiting for those who'd repent[4]—
A gruesome return for the time poorly spent.

When I was late for school or fought with my kin,
It wasn't the scolding—it was the sin.
Hellfire loomed, a torment to dread,
A fate that lingered in every word said.

---

1   1 Thessalonians 5:2, 2 Peter 3:10, Revelation 16:15
2   1 Corinthians 15:51-52
3   Matthew 24:40
4   Revelation 20:4

With such a cost, how could I stray?
"Jesus, stay near me, show me the way."
Yet still, I wonder, trembling with fear,
When You return, will You leave me here?[5]

You say you love me, yet my heart is torn,
Why is Your love so wrapped in scorn?
Is love a noose, or is it a guide?
In Your promise of mercy, do You truly abide?

I long to believe, but the fear runs deep,
Will Your love find me, or will it sweep
Past this flawed and fragile soul?
You say You love me—but is it whole?

---

5   Matthew 7:21-23

Faith the Size of a Mustard Seed

Your word says, with faith as small as a seed,[1]
I could move mountains, fulfill every need.
My faith is strong; it's a flame that won't cease,
Each day begins and ends on my knees.

At school, they mock the prayers I proclaim,
But I stand firm and invoke Your name.[2]
Yet when pain cuts deep, and I call to You,
Why do my mountains refuse to move?

My deafness remains, my cries unheeded,
My loved ones still crippled, their healing still needed.
I scream with conviction, "Grandma, come forth!"[3]
But tomorrow they'll bury her in the cold earth.

What promises Your word so boldly gives!
Yet I've yet to see them where I live.
Faith unshaken, devotion true,
Why do Your miracles pass me through?

---

[1] Matthew 17:20
[2] Matthew 5:11-12
[3] John 11:43

Am I too small, too flawed, too weak?
Is there more faith I still must seek?
Or are the mountains never meant to fall,
A silent lesson within it all?

Your word says faith can move the earth,
But all I've seen is loss since birth.
Still, I pray, though my soul feels hollow,
Hoping one day, Your truth will follow.[4]

---
4 John 8:23

Who Left Who?

Backslidden, they called it—living in sin,
While Jesus stood waiting to welcome me in.[1]
I went through that phase, a pregnant bride,
But the truth is, I never left His side.

From the church—yes, I walked away,
From judgmental walls that led hearts astray.
Void of love, cold and unkind,
Understanding was nowhere to find.

But Jesus? Oh no, He stayed near,
Through every doubt, through every tear.
I spoke to Him daily, His word my guide,
With a cross on my neck, He was always inside.[2]

My walls adorned with gospel art,
His presence remained within my heart.[3]
I prayed with my children, shared His name,
My love for Him burned just the same.

Yes, for a time, I lived in sin,[4]
And wasn't welcome to come back in.

---

1   Luke 15:20
2   Romans 8:38-39
3   I Corinthians 3:16
4   John 8:11; 1 John 2:1

But Jesus and I were still as one,⁵
So tell me now—who left who, then?

Was it me who strayed, or the walls that failed,
When love grew cold and grace derailed?
For I never left his steadfast embrace—
It was the church that fell and forgot His face.

---
5   John 10:28-29

A Holy Home

I RETURNED TO the church when my children were small,
Seeking a place where they'd hear His call.[1]
The love of His Son, a gift to impart,[2]
A gospel foundation to shape their heart.

I couldn't withhold this truth so divine,
So we went back, hand in hand, to align.
To reconnect with a spiritual kin,
To welcome His presence and let grace begin.[3]

We were welcomed, embraced, no questions, no doubt,
A circle of love that wrapped us about.
I made friends, connections, bonds to hold,
A family of faith, more precious than gold.[4]

Now as an adult, the role has shifted,
A provider of love, a soul uplifted.
For my kids, I'll build a holy home,[5]
Where they'll never feel lost, never alone.

---

1 Matthew 19:14
2 Romans 6:23
3 Matthew 18:20
4 Romans 15:7
5 Joshua 24:4

The church is our anchor, the faith we profess,
A haven of peace, a wellspring of rest.
For as they grow, they'll always see,
The love of His Son flowing through me.[6]

---

[6] Matthew 5:16

To the Jew First

"To the Jew first," the call was clear,[1]
A mission that burned, a purpose dear.
I took it to heart, to honor His name,
To share His love, a holy flame.

"To the Jew I became a Jew,"[2]
A verse I cherished, steadfast and true.
Not as a preacher with pointed hand,
But as a friend, walking their land.

I joined the JCC to meet a few,
Attended their events, and soon I grew
Into a name, a face they'd know,
A part of their world, a gentle glow.

No sermons given, no airs of pride,
Just moments shared, side by side.
A whisper of Jesus, soft and sincere,
A love that sought to draw them near.

For love builds bridges, not divides,
A bond that deepens, where truth resides.
"To the Jew first," my heart would yearn,
Not to deceive, but to help them turn.

---

1 Romans 1:16; Romans 2:9-10; Matthew 10:5-6
2 I Corinthians 9:20

A seed of kindness, a hand to extend,
For God's patience knows no end.
I walked their path with care and grace,
Hoping to show them Jesus' embrace.

The Truth I Knew

I WAS A proud Christian, bold in my faith,
Convinced of the truth, of heaven and grace.
The path was clear, the stakes were high,
Without Jesus, the soul would surely die.[1]

"You can't reach God without His Son,"[2]
The simple truth I lived upon.
Reject Him, and Hell would await—
An eternal end, a dire fate.[3]

Somehow, I knew, I must share this light,[4]
Bring His people to Him, day or night.
Through word or deed, in any way,
To guide their hearts, lest they stray.

For Jesus loves them, and so do I,
And love compels, though questions lie.
When you love someone, you want what's best,
To lead them to peace, to eternal rest.

---

1   Revelation 20:15
2   John 14:6
3   John 3:36
4   John 8:12

So I'll carry this truth, this sacred plea,
To help them see what was shown to me.
For love demands, and faith commands,
That I walk with them, hand in hand.

To Serve and to Share

I wanted to teach my children to serve,
A lesson I learned, a value preserved.
As a child, the mission[1] kept me whole,
Grounded my heart, steadied my soul.

In the safety of the church, I found peace,
Jesus embraced me, my fears released.
I want the same for my children's days,
To walk with Him, to know His ways.[2]

This new body of believers we've found,
With a mission to Jews that is profound.
Though we are not Jewish, we choose to learn,
Their culture, traditions, with hearts that yearn.

We dress like them, respect their ways,
Understanding their past, their pain, their days.
For only with love can trust begin,
A bridge of respect to let us in.[3]

---

1   Matthew 28:19-20
2   Proverbs 22:6
3   1 Peter 3:15

And once we're in, with hearts sincere,
We'll share of Jesus, His love so near.
Not with force, but with care and grace,
Inviting them to see His face.

For service is love, and love is the key,[4]
To open their hearts and set them free.
I'll teach my children, as I was taught,
That serving with love is the mission we've sought.

---
4   John 13:34-35

A Careful Cross

I feel a little sorrow, a weight I bear,
That I can't be honest, can't fully share.
With my Jewish friends, I tread with care,
God forbid I offend them, their hearts laid bare.

My love is sincere, my commitment true,
I care for their souls in all that I do.
As a friend, I'll stay, steadfast and kind,
Hiding my beliefs, leaving judgments behind.

Only in moments tender and still,
When I sense they'll listen, perhaps they will.
I'll speak of my faith with gentle grace,
But never too soon, never in haste.

For if I say it outright, they'll surely turn,
A friendship lost, a bridge to burn.
Their space will close, their hearts retreat,
So I keep my cross discreet.

This is the burden, the cross I bear,
To love in silence, to show I care.
Waiting for moments when truth can unfold,
For hearts to soften, for stories told.[1]

---

1   James 5:7-8

Until then, I'll walk this careful line,
A friend in their world, their trust to define.
For love is patient,[2] and faith can wait,
In their time,[3] not mine—this is my fate.

---

2   1 Corinthians 13:4
3   Romans 11:23-24

The Language of Love

The language we use when speaking to Jews
Demands great care, the right words to choose.
Not to offend, but to build a bridge,
To guide their hearts to the gospel's ridge.

"Jesus Christ" does not warm their soul,
So Yeshua—His Hebrew name—took its role.
To "convert" is a word they deeply resist,
So "fulfilled" became the term on my list.

Not "church," but a "meeting of Bible believers,"
Softening words, gentle receivers.
Each phrase a step, each word a key,
Unlocking trust with humility.

At first, these terms felt foreign and strange,
But I made it my mission to adapt and change.
For the calling was vital, the purpose true,
To show His love to every Jew.

With time, these words became my own,
A natural language, a seed I'd sown.
Because the mission demands our heart and care,
To speak their language, to meet them there.

For words hold power, they build or divide,
And love is the language where truth can reside.
So I'll speak as they do, and do as they do,
To lead them gently to Yeshua's view.

A TRAINING MANUAL ON...
HOW TO SHARE THE MESSIAH

BY MANNY BROTMAN
President
The Messianic Jewish
Movement International

"And unto the Jews
I became as a Jew,
that I might gain the Jews"
- I Corinthians 9:20

CONTENTS

		Page
I.	WHAT IS THE PURPOSE OF THIS TRAINING?	1
II.	HOW CAN YOU HELP YOUR JEWISH FRIEND *TO PRAY* WITH YOU TO INVITE THE MESSIAH INTO HIS HEART AND LIFE?	1
III.	HOW CAN YOU *UNDERSTAND* YOUR JEWISH FRIEND?	1
IV.	HOW CAN YOU *AVOID* THAT WHICH WILL KEEP YOUR JEWISH FRIEND *AWAY* FROM THE MESSIAH?	4
V.	WHAT CAN YOU *EMPHASIZE* TO *DRAW* YOUR JEWISH FRIEND TO HIS MESSIAH?	5
VI.	HOW CAN YOU *CREATE AN INTEREST* IN *SPIRITUAL THINGS*?	7
VII.	HOW CAN YOU HELP YOUR JEWISH FRIEND *TO WANT* "WHAT YOU AND OTHERS HAVE!"	9
VIII.	HOW CAN YOU *CLEARLY* EXPLAIN THE PLAN OF ATONEMENT IN THE MESSIAH?	9
IX.	HOW CAN YOU EFFECTIVELY *FOLLOW-UP* WITH YOUR JEWISH FRIEND?	11
X.	HOW CAN YOU *ANSWER* YOUR JEWISH FRIEND'S QUESTIONS?	13

MESSIANIC SOUL-WINNER'S CARD
"The fruit of the righteous is a tree of life, and he that wins souls is wise!" – Proverbs 11:30

A. BECOME "AS A JEW, TO THE JEWS!" (1 Cor. 9:20)

DO SAY	DON'T SAY
(1) MESSIAH YESHUA, MESSIAH JESUS, THE MESSIAH	(1) JESUS CHRIST
(2) MESSIANIC JEW, COMPLETED JEW, FULFILLED JEW	(2) CONVERT
(3) A BIBLE BELIEVER	(3) A CHRISTIAN
(4) COME TO A MEETING OF BIBLE BELIEVERS	(4) COME TO CHURCH
(5) 2ND PART OF BIBLE, NEW COVENANT	(5) NEW TESTAMENT
(6) TREE, EXECUTION STAKE	(6) CROSS

EXPLANATION

(1) The term "CHRIST" does NOT have ANY Jewish connotation to the average Jew.
(2) "Convert" means to TAKE AWAY Judaism and to become a "goy," a Gentile. "MESSIANIC JEW" means to BUILD UPON OR ADD TO his Jewish heritage by *gaining* the atonement, *gaining* the Messiah and *GAINING A MORE PERSONAL RELATIONSHIP WITH GOD!* He does not have to give up his wonderful Biblical Jewish heritage. Emphasize what he gains!
(3) ALL non-Jews are considered CHRISTIANS, even Hitler.
(4) The term "CHURCH" is too Gentile to be desirable to a Jewish person.
(5) "New Testament" is considered a NON-JEWISH book. *Don't emphasize its name.* USE IT!
(6) The "CROSS" has been a symbol of Jewish persecution for centuries.

The Fascination of Faith

The Orthodox world fascinates me so,
With rituals and traditions I barely know.
Obsessed with rules, their devotion profound,
G-d is central, in all they're bound.[1]

It blows my mind, their disciplined ways,
The smallest things sacred throughout their days.
Every action, a holy decree,
A life of detail, a mystery to me.

Yet without Yeshua, I feel the void,
A longing unfulfilled, a joy destroyed.
For all their rituals, their sacred lore,
Without salvation, it's an unopened door.[2]

How beautiful, how bright it would be,
To show them the grace that set me free.
To lead one soul to His embrace,
To witness the light upon their face.

---

1 Romans 10:2
2 Acts 4:12

Their faith is strong, their hearts sincere,
But there's a love they've yet to hear.[3]
A bridge between their world and mine,
A hope that G-d's love will intertwine.

Oh, to bring one into His care,
To see them find the answer there.
The Orthodox world, a wonder to see,
But complete with Yeshua—it's destiny.[4]

---

3 2 Corinthians 3:15-16
4 Romans 10:4

The Mission to Reach

To reach Jews for Jesus has been so clear,
A simple path, no need for fear.
Show them their sins can be wiped away,
And Jesus will love them, come what may.

They can still eat falafel, keep tradition alive,
As long as they let His grace inside.
Many have listened, their hearts made new,
But the Orthodox? They've a different view.

Obsessed with their texts, each letter, each line,
As if proof alone could make them align.
So I set out to show them, bold and unshaken,
How Jesus is present in every word taken.

Not with deceit, but with truth I came,
Pointing to scripture, calling His name.
"I'm right, you're wrong—just look and you'll see!"
But their laughter echoed, mocking me.

"Your verses don't match, they're out of context,
Mistranslated words, or ideas perplexed."
They discarded my proof, but still, I pressed,
Determined to help them see they're blessed.

Their hearts are hard, their pride runs deep,
But for their souls, I will not sleep.
The mission remains, unwavering, strong,
To help them see where they belong.

For truth is patient, love endures,
And one day, perhaps, their faith ensures,
That their laughter fades, their hearts agree,
And the light of Yeshua sets them free.

A Vessel for Your Will

Dear L-rd, please use me, Your vessel, Your voice,
To show the Jews Your love, Your choice.
I'll study intensely, as I did in my youth,
I'll learn the Hebrew, to show them the truth.[1]

Not just a verse, but chapters I'll know,
If it takes the whole Tanach, help me – I'll grow.
I'm committed, Lord, I give my all,
To answer Your mission, to heed Your call.

Please, Lord, lift the veil from their eyes,[2]
Reveal your light, so they realize.
I'll do what it takes, I'm ready, I'm strong,
To bring them home, where they belong.

One day we'll hear, in voices loud,
"Blessed is He," they'll cry out – proud.[3]
In Your name, they'll find their rest,
With hearts redeemed, their lives are blessed.

---

1   2 Timothy 2:15
2   2 Corinthians 3:15-16
3   Matthew 23:39

Your second coming,[4] Lord, I long to see,
In my lifetime, let it be.
I pray with fervor, my heart laid bare,
Use me, O Lord, to bring them there.[5]

---

4   Revelation 22:20
5   Matthew 9:37-38

Come Wrestle with Me

These Orthodox Jews, so difficult, so bold,
They spoke with knowledge, with truths untold.
I thought I knew the Bible, clear and plain,
But their words brought doubt, their questions, pain.

I came prepared, my answers sure,
Yet each response made me less secure.
The words of a rabbi, tapes played through,
Brought cracks to my faith, as doubts slowly grew.

Isaiah 53,[1] my rock, my stay,
Even that was swept away.
Prophecies in Matthew, once so bright,
Were halved and altered—was this still right?

Bible tampering, translations skewed,
What seemed so clear now misconstrued.
Could my foundation, my core, my truth,
Be a tower crumbling in pursuit?[2]

---

1   Isaiah 53:3-5
2   Psalm 11:3

This can't be. Please, it cannot be so,
Everything I've ever known, my soul's bedrock below,
Its lifeblood, its purpose, its sacred flow.
Could it all unravel? Let it not be so!

Yet in this storm, this anguished plea,
Truth whispers softly: "Come, wrestle with me."
For faith that stands must face the fire,
To burn away what's false, and rise higher.[3]

---

[3] Zechariah 13:9

Let's Get Biblical

I was warned against the path I chose,
By voices fervent, with warnings that rose.
"Stay clear," they said, "of Rabbi Singer's snare,
His words are traps; tread not there."[1]

But curiosity lit a fire in me,
A desire to grow, to learn, to see.[2]
For my faith was strong, unshakable, whole—
How could truth ever fracture my soul?

"Let's Get Biblical," the title proclaimed,
A challenge issued, my spirit inflamed.
To know my Bible, to sharpen my view,
To stand firm when questions grew.

I listened, I studied, I dug deep.
The words cut through like wounds that seep.
No magic tricks, no subtle deceit,
Just an open text, laid bare at my feet.

"See it yourself," the rabbi would say,
"Check the context, don't look away."
What I found in the pages, stark and clear,
Caused trembling hands and rising fear.

---

[1] Colossians 2:8
[2] Proverbs 25:2

Mistranslations, distortions, a tangled weave,
A faith I'd cherished, hard to believe.
My world unraveled, foundations shook,
Truth direct from the People of the Book.

An atomic bomb of revelation fell,
A truth that shattered my fortress shell.
Not with coercion, nor whispers sly,
But with what was written, plain to the eye.

Oh, how the pain of truth can rend,[3]
A life reformed, but not at its end.
For though the journey has brought its strife,
It carved out space for a fuller life.

Let's get biblical, the rabbi dared,
And through the fire, my soul was bared.[4]
Not lost, but seeking, not gone, but new,
A path that honors what's wholly true.[5]

---

3   Psalm 119:130
4   Psalm 12:6
5   Psalm 34:14

The Silent Struggle

In silence, I wrestle, alone in the night,
A crisis of faith—no hope, no light.[1]
This isn't just belief; it's my very life,
My core, my heart, my identity's strife.

The texts are clear, their truth laid bare,
But to voice it aloud—how could I dare?
Who would believe me, who could I tell,
That my faith now feels like a fragile shell?

I've never known such despair, such fear,
But Jesus is with me—wait, are you here?[2]
Were you ever there, this voice in my mind?
Who have I prayed to, and trusted in kind?

It's too much to bear, this weight, this doubt,
That presence within I can't live without.
I'm scared to speak, to let anyone see,
Yet the facts before me demand honesty.

---

1 Psalm 22:1-2
2 Lamentations 3:40-41

Alone in this battle, afraid yet awake,
I stand on the edge of the truths I must take.
For though I am trembling, lost in the fray,
The search for what's real won't let me stay.[3]

---

[3] Psalm 42:5-6

The Silent Departure

This crisis of faith, too heavy to bear,
I reached for a friend, for someone to care.
With trembling hands, my heart laid bare,
I thought she'd embrace me, but silence was there.[1]

Through tears, I spoke of the doubts I've known,
Of Jesus rejected, a path overthrown.
But instead of comfort, she turned away,
Uncertain, afraid of what I had to say.

"It's okay," I whispered, "we'll be alright.
No matter my journey, we'll share the light.
If I stop going to church, we'll still meet,
For coffee, for laughter, for moments sweet."

"I'll dance at your wedding; I'll stand by your side,
Through joy, through love, through tears we've cried."
But my words hung heavy, unanswered, undone,
And her silence cut deeper than anyone's.[2]

She left, not in anger, but in quiet despair,
A friendship suspended, left hanging there…[3]

---

1   Psalm 38:11
2   Psalm 55:12-14
3   Psalm 41:9

When Love Turns to Hate

It didn't take long for the whispers to grow,
For the pastor's memo to let everyone know.
Verses were quoted, sharp as a knife:
"One who denies Christ is the Antichrist."[1]

The message was clear, the judgment severe:
I was the devil they all came to fear.[2]
"Do not welcome, do not let them stay,[3]
Turn them away, keep evil at bay."[4]

My friendships dissolved, like smoke in the air,
The bond we shattered, replaced with despair.
A wedding—a moment I promised to share—
Now closed to me, told I couldn't be there.

How can relationships end so cold?
People I loved, now distant, now old.
Closer than family, or so it had seemed,
But now I'm the shadow in their brightest dreams.

---

1   I John 2:22
2   2 John 1:10-11
3   1 John 2:19
4   Romans 16:17

A Jew, they say, just doesn't know,
But an apostate chooses the path below.[1]
No redemption, no grace, no second chance,
Only rejection, a severed stance.[2]

This isn't the love I was taught to believe,
Unconditional warmth that never would leave.
But here I am, in this foreign place,
Their love turned to hate, a bitter disgrace.

I never imagined to take this road,
To carry this weight, this painful load.
But truth, once seen, can't be undone—
Even if it leaves you the forsaken one.[3]

---

1   2 Corinthians 6:14-17
2   Titus 3:10-11
3   Psalm 27:10

Shattered and Free

When I walked out of the church, one thing I knew,
I would be alone on this path forged anew.

But truth demands action, and I could not stay;
Lies and betrayal would eat me away.

One last time, I sat in the pew,
Praying to God, *What should I do?*

This place, once a haven, now felt unkind,
Every thought, every word, a betrayal confined.

For friends and community, I tried to remain,
But if they can't accept, why endure the pain?
If they'll hate me and loathe me, I cannot delay—
I must forge ahead and find my own way.[4]

An apostate's fate, no turning back,
Each step forward widens the track.
The verses they read during service that day,
Pierced my heart in an excruciating way.

---

[4] Isaiah 66:5

In anguish, I threw the Bible down on the pew,
Unintentionally, it fell, its weight breaking through.

As did my heart as I raced out the door,
Shattered and heavy, yet craving more.

Yet even in silence, I heard it resound:
A voice of conviction, steadfast and profound.
Though alone in the moment, my soul understood—
To betray myself would do me no good.[1]

So I rise from the pew and step through the door,
I am not alone—I am something more.[2]

---

1   Deuteronomy 31:6
2   Psalm 119:30

An Exodus

As I left those giant sanctuary doors,
It felt like the sea being split just for me.
Through the desert, alone, in the vast unknown,
I'd have to find my place, on my own. [1]

But as I forged this path, others were there—
I was not alone; footprints marked where
Others had tread, their stories untold,
Guiding my journey with courage bold. [2]

One by one, I met them—each the same tale:
Of discovering truth, of lifting the veil.
They called themselves by different names:
Bnei Noach, Noahides, righteous flames.

But their stories were like déjà vu,
A shared history, a journey so true.
Though we'd walked alone, we found each other,
And in that bond, my heart discovered

Comfort, validation, confirmation deep—
A kinship awakened, a joy to keep.

---

1 Genesis 12:1
2 Isaiah 42:16

As I continued, the groups I met grew,
Hundreds, then thousands—who knew?
Some chose conversion, some stayed as they are,
Kindred soulmates, each a guiding star.[3]

I'm blessed now to have two families strong—
A Jew and a part of a swelling throng.
But also connected to those who belong
To this shared journey, this sacred song.

---

3   Isaiah 56:3-5

Homecoming

The deeper I delved into Christianity,
The more it unraveled,
Each thread pulling at the foundation
Of all I once believed.[1]

Certainties crumbled,
Walls I leaned on for years
Fell to dust.
But then, I turned to the Torah.[2]

At first, a spark,
Then a steady flame
Illuminating truths
I had long sought in shadow.

The deeper I studied,
The more it unfolded,
A tapestry of meaning,
Layer upon layer of wisdom,
Patiently waiting to be seen.

---

1 Jeremiah 16:19
2 Psalm 19:7-8

Since my youth,
The Bible was a riddle,
Words blurred by struggle,
Stories clouded by doubt.
But now—
Oh, how it reads so clear,[3]

So easily,
As if it always knew
The lens I needed to see.
Without the filter,
It all came together—

Simple,
Elementary,
Yet profound.
The mitzvot:[4]
Once dismissed as hollow,
Now reveal their beauty.

---

3   Isaiah 29:18
4   Proverbs 6:23

Each one, a gem of meaning,
A purpose woven into life itself.
Not empty,
But brimming with truth,
Each act, a step closer to wholeness.

The more I learned,
The more I yearned—
To do, to live,
To weave these teachings
Into the fabric of my being.
This is what my soul craved,[1]
What my children deserve,
What I had been searching for all along.
This is home.
This is peace.
This is purpose.[2]

---

1 Psalm 42:1-2
2 Isaiah 55:1

How Long Can This Last?

I keep going, just me,
Learning wherever I could be free.
I could never tell my parents. No way!
I love them too much to ruin their day.

They think I'm still spreading the word,
My time with Jews is a mission, to think otherwise–absurd.
To them, it's a plan to reach the Jews,
If they only knew, it would break them in two.

When they visit, I scramble, I hide,
Jewish books backward, Hebrew pushed aside.
I smile, I nod, I play my part,
But it's getting harder to guard my heart.[1]

How long can I keep on living this lie?[2]
Pretending, deflecting, just getting by.
I don't want to hurt them, but this isn't me,
And someday, the truth might need to break free.

---

1 Ecclesiastes 3:7
2 Psalm 119:29

A Friday Night I'll Never Forget

A Friday night I'll never forget—Shabbat,
The air thick with stillness, my phone off,
 my thoughts caught.
After the service, a message from my father:
"I'm coming over," - unexpected - "I won't be a bother".

Oh no! My study, my sanctuary exposed!
Every translation, every secret I'd composed.
Laid bare on the table, my notes in the open,
Each question I'd hidden, each word unspoken.

He arrived before me, sitting tall in a chair,
My father, my guide, now sifting through my despair.
"Come here," he called, his tone edged with concern,
And suddenly, I was a child—my stomach churned.

"It hasn't gone unnoticed—I see you've changed,
The way you eat, the way you dress—it's strange.
I know what's happening; I see it in your face.
You've joined a cult, lost in some misguided space."

"No, Dad, please," I begged, "just let me explain—
It's questions I've asked, truths I've sought to attain.
The answers I found led me here, to this place.
It's not what you think, I've not fallen from grace."[1]

He sighed and promised, "We'll learn together.
I'll guide you back; I'll make it better."
But when I showed him my notes, my search, my path,
His certainty faltered in the aftermath.

That night, he sought answers, stayed up until three,
The rabbi's voice echoing, questions breaking free.
At my door, he knocked, his face ashen and pale,
"What I thought was truth," he whispered, "has failed."

He sat on my bed, his stare hollow and wide,
"I tried, but the texts—they don't coincide.
The rabbi is right, the Jews—they hold the key.
But what does it mean, and what now for me?"

The rug pulled out, his faith unraveled,
A minister lost, a father baffled.
"I can't convert; I'm too old to change.
But I'll honor this truth, though it feels so strange.

A righteous gentile, a Ben Noach I'll be,
Walking my path, still tethered to thee."
And so that night, a journey began—
Two souls wandering, yet hand in hand.

---

1   1 Samuel 3:15–18

The Elephant in the Room

Telling mom was like unraveling threads,
Words caught in the space between breaths.
"It's like The Matrix," I tried to explain,
The red pill taken, the plug pulled away.

But her world was steady, unshaken, whole.
"This is what I've always known," her truth she told.
"Plug me back in," she whispered, afraid—
For her, my choices felt like a blade.

She wept for my soul, for her fears made real,
For grandchildren swept in the tide I feel.
Her pain cut deeper than I could foresee,
And then she said, "You've destroyed our family."

Extreme? I argued, but truth can sting—
Traditions now torn, not a small thing.
Kosher made the table a battlefield,
Thanksgiving blessings left unrevealed.

Christmas? No. Easter? Hard to defend—
Even coffee became a line to bend.
And in her eyes, her words still hung,
A sorrowful song I'd left unsung.

But time, the healer, brought her near,
Her love surviving through pain and fear.
Now we meet, though silence looms—
The elephant waits in quiet rooms.

And that's okay—we've found our way,
In love and respect, we choose to stay.
Though she will always pray for my soul,
She's still here and that fills a hole.

Dizzy with Discovery

So much to learn,
A mountain of wisdom, towering, endless.
Blessings for every food—
Before, after, in gratitude's rhythm,
Each bite a sacred moment,
Each taste a chance to connect.

Prayers—
Words that shape the day,
Morning, afternoon, night,
A heartbeat of devotion,
A melody of intention.

How to dress,
Modesty woven into the fabric of life,
Each thread a reminder,
Each choice a reflection.

Kosher—
what's in, what's out,
A careful dance with every meal,
Five sets of dishes,
A choreography of care,
Sacred lines drawn in the everyday.

Hebrew—
The sacred language of the Jews,
Letters that breathe history,
Words that form worlds.
Each syllable a prayer,
Each phrase a connection
To those who walked this path before me.

The Parsha—
Uniting us week by week,
A shared journey, a shared story,
Timeless lessons unfolding anew,
Binding hearts across generations.

So much to learn—
It spins my mind,
A whirlwind of mitzvot and meaning.
Not enough hours in the day,
Not enough moments to grasp it all.
Yet within the dizziness,
A steady pull,

A quiet joy—
For each new step I take
Is a step closer to something eternal.

What Have I Done?

WHAT HAVE I done, with words untrue,
I fractured hearts, broke trust in two.
Jews opened wide their souls to me,
Yet I deceived, though unintentionally.

My ways were wrong, not kind nor clear,
A shadow cast by guilt and fear.
I veiled my lies in holy guise,
Believing love could justify.

I thought they sought redeeming grace,
But lost their trust within my embrace.
How many lives did I misguide?
How many tears from those who tried?

Now I must rebuild what I betrayed,
With truth and light, no debts unpaid.
To heal the wounds, restore the torn,
A humbler heart must be reborn.

For in their eyes, I see the cost—
The weight of faith so deeply lost.
I cannot change what's come to pass,
But love, sincere, can heal at last.

To make things right, I'll tread this ground,
With quiet steps, no boastful sound.
A path of penance, slow and true,
Until my heart is proven new.

The Three Times

Rejecting three times—it's a real thing,
A test of resolve, of what yearning can bring.
I annoyed my new Jewish friends, it's true,
With questions unending, my hunger grew.

"We're not religious," they'd kindly explain,
"If you're so obsessed, find someone who can."
After a Friday night Shabbaton's glow,
I saw a light at Chabad, burning low.

It was late, but the pull was strong and real,
I needed to know, to share, to feel.
I walked in, heart racing, a little afraid,
To speak to the rabbi, my case to be made.

"I want to convert," I declared with fire.
"Impossible," he said, dashing desire.
"You can't be a Jew, as I can't be a dame.
We all have our place; yours isn't the same."

"Can I come and learn from you?" I tried.
"No, you can't. You're not on this side."
I left disheartened, the words struck deep,
A rejection that lingered, a pain to keep.

But I didn't stop—I wouldn't give in,
Again and again, I returned to him.
With arguments, passion, my plea made clear,
Let me in, Rabbi. Let me draw near.

More than three times, the answer was "No,"
But still, I persisted, refused to let go.
Until one visit, the tone rearranged,
"My great-grandmother," I said, "This could change."

Her grave in a Jewish cemetery lay,
Could he help me learn of her life, her way?
"This changes things," he said with care,
A shift in the air, a bridge to repair.

"While you search, you can attend my class.
Torah and Parsha—come, time will pass."
The door, once locked, now open a crack,
A journey began, no turning back.

Rejecting three times—it's a real thing,
But persistence can make a new beginning sing.
Through questions and trials, the path became clear,
A story of faith, of longing, and near.

Knocking Again

THE RABBIS SAID, There's no need for more.
Stay as you are; don't open this door.
Be a Bat Noach; it's easier so,
Fewer struggles, less weight to tow.

Unlike the others, we don't decree
That heaven demands you must be like me.
Your path is clear, your soul complete,
No need for a Jew's unsteady feet.

To be a Jew is a burdened fight,
613 mitzvot, both day and night.
We're hated, beloved, then hated once more,
Our fate is heavy, our trials unsure.

Better for you to stay where you stand.
Learn Torah, seek truth, but understand—
This battle isn't yours to take,
No need for a choice that makes hearts break.

But I pleaded, No, this isn't my way.
You don't see the fire that won't go away.
This advice may be wise for another soul,
But my spirit demands a different goal.

You say, Turn back, no need to pursue,
But I cannot settle; I must be a Jew.
There's something inside that will not rest,
A voice that calls me to this test.

So close the door, turn me away,
Say "Not today, not today".
But I'll be here, knocking still,
With steady hands and unshaken will.

You'll push me back, again and again,
But I'll return, the same refrain:
Until you accept what I've always known—
That this is my path, my heart, my home.

Determined to Grow

I was determined to fit in, to learn,
To speak as they speak, to follow, to turn.
A stranger in a world both ancient and new,
Where whispers of wisdom thread stories through.

The Parsha each week—a melody unknown,
Stories I'd heard, but now richly grown.
Layers unraveled, meanings profound,
In this sacred cycle, my soul was unbound.

Uncomfortable moments, a seat out of place,
The awkward non-Jew in this hallowed space.
Reading in English, my questions unending,
Eager for truths their teachings were lending.

Grateful for patience, for kindness bestowed,
For those who lightened the weight I owed.
They saw my errors, yet softly steered,
Never lashing at missteps feared.

Touching the wine, a light switch aglow,
Mistakes of an outsider longing to know.
Yet hands reached out, teaching with care,
Inviting me deeper, to simply be there.

I was determined to learn, to learn to belong,
To hum their prayers, to join in their song.
And though I still stumble, my heart's intent true,
I've found a new home here, though not born a Jew.

The Beit Din

I HAD WRITTEN the Beit Din, my heart in my pen,
But silence met my words time and again.
"Be patient," I whispered, though time seemed to stall,
Caught in a limbo, no answers at all.

I feared to be seen as a nudge, a pest,
Yet the waiting gnawed deeply, a weight in my chest.
Life hung suspended, uncertain, unsure,
A door I was knocking, yet none opened the door.

At last, I decided, there's nothing to lose,
So again I reached out, my words to peruse.
A few more letters, a heartfelt plea,
Hoping they'd hear the depth of my need.

And then I learned, persistence was key,
Rejected, ignored, yet steadfast was me.
They wanted to see the strength of my will,
To prove my resolve, unwavering, still.

At last, they accepted; the process began,
A meeting, a future, a long-awaited plan.
The journey had started, the path now clear,
Finally on my way, shedding the fear.

In patience and struggle, I found my own voice,
A test of my spirit, my unwavering choice.
What once seemed denied, was never in vain,
Each step now treasured, born of the strain.

Longing to Belong

A Pesach table, a guest of a guest,
A seat offered warmly, but unaware of the rest.
The host unknowing, the rules unclear,
A non-Jew in attendance, my presence sincere.

The Seder delayed, whispers filled the room,
Several assembled, their faces in gloom.
Unbeknownst to me, I had sparked a debate,
A question of law, a matter of fate.

Embarrassed, I sat as the moments dragged by,
The hold-up was me, and I wanted to cry.
A rabbi decided, "It's permitted, it's fine,"
But even his tone carried a chastising line.

Then came the instructions, each step laid out,
Who pours for whom? A new round of doubt.
On Pesach night, someone else pours for you,
But called out again—"What now should we do?"

Touching the wine, a source of distress,
A rule I had broken, though I couldn't have guessed.
Another meal, another mistake,
An open bottle passed, another delay to take.

Humiliation, sharp, at the center I stood,
The "problem" was me, though my heart meant good.
Another rabbi consulted, another meal stalled,
The non-Jew, again, the one who's called.

I wish they'd learn, take a moment to care,
To see the *ger* with compassion laid bare.
For the Torah commands to welcome, not shame,
Yet too often the burden feels one and the same.

I just want to fit in, to be part of this space,
Not a source of discomfort, not out of place.
A seat at the table, a voice in the song,
To simply be here, and know I belong.

Flaws and All

EVERY GROUP HAS their nuts, their flaws, their cracks,
No people immune, no virtues intact.
I made the mistake of a pedestal high,
Believing each Jew was pure as the sky.

I thought they'd all understand, all be good,
Trusted too deeply, more than I should.
It was them I admired, their lives I esteemed,
To be one of them was the life that I dreamed.

The title "rabbi"—revered, divine,
A guide to the sacred, a teacher of time.
But even among them, I found the truth grim,
Some rabbis stray from the light within.

I learned every group has its shadows, its shame,
People who falter, who tarnish the name.
Compassion does not fill every Jewish heart,
Even among them, darkness takes part.

The lesson was bitter, the pain runs deep,
The details I bury, in silence they sleep.
Yet through the hurt, one truth remains clear:
It's the Torah I follow, what drew me here.

Not for the people, flawed as they are,
But for the wisdom, the truth, David's star.
I chose this path for what it bestows,
Not for perfection in those it knows.

Thank You

I SO APPRECIATE the ones who cared,
The ones who helped me when I despaired.
They stood beside me, steady and true,
Guiding my steps, showing me what to do.

They taught me kashrut, the sacred way,
How to *bentsch*, to bless, to give thanks each day.
And most of all, they taught me to hear—
The countless opinions, both far and near.

Michael and Susan, forever tall,
In their beliefs, convictions, and all.
Michael, a fighter with fire in his tone,
A loud New Yorker, with opinions his own.

He'd stand for justice, defend the weak,
Small in stature, but fierce when he'd speak.
A whirlwind of passion, never backing down,
With a heart so big, it wore no frown.

Susan, sweet Susan, a Southern delight,
With kindness and love, she made things right.
A nurturing soul, accepting and warm,
She brought calm amidst every storm.

Together they taught me, lifted me high,
When my path was unclear, they helped me try.
To Michael and Susan, I owe so much—
Your guidance, your care, your heartfelt touch.

Thank you for standing, for holding my hand,
For teaching conviction and love for this land.
For being the ones who saw me through,
Michael and Susan, I thank you.

Don't Touch the Wine

Don't touch the wine!
Did I make that clear before?
A rule so simple, yet it holds the weight
Of something much, much more.

I learned it the hard way,
Through heartache and regret,
A lesson wrapped in ancient threads
I won't soon forget.

So much surrounds that bottle—
A symbol, a line, a wall.
Its purpose whispers centuries,
But its impact can feel so small.

For the one who reaches unknowing,
Or the one who stumbles near,
It's not just about the wine itself,
It's about what they hold dear.

It's not the liquid, not the taste,
Not the vintage or the year.
It's the sanctity, the guarded space,
The boundary kept so clear.

And yet, perhaps, we miss the mark,
In how we teach and share.
To extend the lesson without the sting,
To guide with love and care.

It would do us good to handle this,
With wisdom and with grace,
To honor tradition, but never forget
The humanity in its place.

So don't touch the wine!
Yes, the rule must stand.
But let's not forget the soul who learns,
Or the warmth of an outstretched hand.

Limbo Ends

Forever in limbo, the waiting endured,
Meetings with the Beit Din, rare and obscured.
Begging and pleading for each step ahead,
Patience stretched thin, hope hanging by a thread.

Each step closer revealed yet more to bear,
Another hurdle, another snare.
Year after year, the questions arose,
Concerns multiplying, new trials to compose.

My children's status, their tender age,
Scholarships needed, another page.
A single mom—a case too complex,
Our commitment questioned, our faith to test.

Four years long, a journey so steep,
Significant growth, moments to weep.
Two little hearts, their leaps profound,
While I held steady, earthward, unbound.

But we did it—my children and me,
Through trials and waiting, through uncertainty.
The last Beit Din, the final decree,
In Eretz Yisrael, where my heart longed to be.

A place of promise, a land of light,
Where dreams took form, where faith took flight.
Four years of struggle, but now we belong,
Together, at last, in the land of our song.

Giants of Torah

Three giants in Torah, pillars of the land,
I stood before them, trembling and nervous hands.
Their questions came, familiar, yet profound,
Each answer I gave felt sacred, sound.

Inspiration filled me, commitment in my tone,
But deep within, I felt the unknown.
Scared. Excited. Emotional. Surreal.
Was this moment of truth truly real?

Then came their words, steady and kind,
"Cover your eyes, let your heart align."
Alone I spoke the sacred Shema,
The mantra of a Jew, declaring God's awe.

With those words, they welcomed me in,
"Mazel Tov," they said, my new life would begin.
Now one final step, the mikvah's embrace,
And I'll be a Jew, in my rightful place.

Rabbi Yisrael Rozen

Rabbi Yisrael Rozen, a giant in my eyes,
Probing gently, he asked why I saw this life as a prize?
Was I ready to become a Jew?
Would my children know what's pure and true?

Would I marry a man who fears God's name?
Would I keep a home that honors the same?
Personal matters, both great and small,
He guided me through them, with love through it all.

His questions pierced but were wrapped in care,
Each word a ladder, helping me to prepare.
And when we finished, his smile shone bright,
A beacon of pride, a radiant light.

Proud of the journey my family had faced,
Both spoken trials and those untraced.
He knew the struggles still yet to come,
But his faith in us was unshaken, strong.

A tower of strength for the land of Israel,
Head of Tzomet, a soul so integral.
A member of the rabbinate, a guiding flame,
He carried the weight of Israel's name.

And yet, he took the time to see,
To guide and nurture my family and me.
He saw our potential, our faith, our fight,
And blessed our future with his guiding light.

Rabbi Yisrael Rozen, my hero true,
I owe so much of my journey to you.
Your wisdom, your care, your enduring belief,
Have brought us strength, have brought us peace.

The Mikvah

The mikvah, a ritual foreign and strange,
Yet I knew its waters would mark the change.
A bond with God, a covenant sealed,
A heart transformed, a soul revealed.

From this day forward, I'd be someone new,
Cleansed of my past, with a purpose true.
Forging a path with this family divine,
Their story, their fate, now also mine.

Whether the fate of the Jews is good or grim,
I cast my lot, my life with them.
Their joys, their trials, their ancient fight,
Are now my own, my guiding light.

With that thought, I let the waters surround,
A sacred embrace, a moment profound.
From this day forward, fresh and true,
A new beginning, all things anew.

A New Life, A New Family

As I came out of the waters, I felt the change,
A shift within, profound and strange.
But what followed next took my breath away,
A moment I'll cherish every day.

Three rabbis stood, quiet and proud,
Serious faces, no words aloud.
A table before them, wine set to pour,
Glasses waiting—and then something more.

Wine! I stepped back, instinctive and quick,
But this time, no boundary, no invisible stick.
The bottle was handed directly to me,
What is this moment? Could it truly be?

"Pour for us all." Their words were so kind,
A new realization flooded my mind.
I could touch, I could pour, because now it's true—
I was no longer apart—I was a Jew.

Then they raised their glasses and asked with a grin,
"Make the bracha, let it begin."
With trembling voice, I recited it clear,
And they all said, Amen!—I fought back a tear.

Do you know what that means, that sacred reply?
My bracha counted for them—it wasn't just mine!
No longer a stranger, no longer apart,
Accepted fully, with all of my heart.

My soul was soaring, my heart ablaze,
A new family, new life, in so many ways.
The hurdles were passed, the bond now complete,
With love overflowing, my joy was sweet.

Under the Chuppah in Hebron

One year later, I returned to the land,
With a man who lovingly asked for my hand.
Under the chuppah, with my children near,
Family surrounding, their love so clear.

The sacred place for this joyous simcha—
Hebron, the resting place of Ima and Abba.
Avraham and Sarah, our forebears divine,
Their blessings felt in this moment, mine.

Each sacred ritual, a piece of my story,
More than a wedding, it spoke of God's glory.
My life emerging, renewed and whole,
With every blessing, a lift to my soul.

We danced in circles, laughter and song,
A holy place where we all belong.
The joy was endless, the love profound,
In Hebron's heart, holiness crowned.

A sacred event in a holy space,
Under the chuppah, surrounded by grace.
A new chapter written, a dream come true,
In the land of our fathers, my life was made new.

A Wound, A Gift

My husband's mother came to stay,
Just for a while—she'd heal, then stray.
Her wound was cleaned, the bandage tight,
Showers took care, but we made it right.

Morning coffee, warm and sweet,
Shabbat meals where hands would meet.
She watched my children test my grace,
Saw my struggles, knew my place.

And when my husband caused dismay,
She'd smile and say, "His father was the same way."
Through doctor visits, tests, and scans,
We worked to heal with careful hands.

Yet days turned weeks, and months turned years,
Through laughter shared and wiped-back tears.
A teacher, friend—a hand so wise,
With a loving heart and knowing eyes.

She showed me how a home should glow,
With Shabbat candles, warm and slow.
The songs, the prayers, the sacred light,
Jewish priorities shining bright.

She taught me things I'd never known,
How to create a Jewish home.
Not just the meals, not just the rest,
But building a life with faith as its crest.

She became the Yiddishe Mame I never had,
Through joy and struggle, through good and bad.
And though they thought she stayed to mend,
It was my heart she'd help transcend.

I thought she came so I could care,
To heal her wound with love to spare.
But looking back, now I see—
Hashem had sent her here for me.

She filled a space I didn't know,
She helped me heal, she helped me grow.

A New Chapter in the Promised Land

NOT LONG AFTER, another chapter began,
Our journey led us to this ancient land.
Hopes and dreams in every breath,
A place to live, to love, to rest.

The land of promise, of stories untold,
Of prophets and kings, of courage bold.
Once foreign, distant, a place unknown,
Now it felt like ours—our home.

The soil beneath, the air so sweet,
Every step felt like history beneath our feet.
The echoes of prayers, the songs of old,
Woven with dreams, both new and bold.

We came with hope, with hearts set free,
To build a life, a destiny.
A land no longer in stranger's hand,
But home at last, the Promised Land.

Pinch Me

Pinch me. Is it real?
On a major highway, just outside its walls,
a herd of sheep blocks the traffic light.
Behind them, a robed man with a staff strides slowly.
It feels surreal—
the Bible merging with the modern world
as I wait in my car,
watching time stand still.
Pinch me. This doesn't feel real.
Walking the paved streets of Jaffa,
along the quiet train tracks,
there's a strange peace
woven with the lively hum of a busy city.
Zion Square.
A place full of life,
where on a Thursday night,
some might claim there's no holiness.
But I beg to differ.
Jewish youth—every kind.
Religious. Not religious.
Yerushalmi, immigrants, sabras.
Some who came from distant lands,
others who've never left this soil.
Singing. Dancing. Debating.

Here, in this unlikely chaos,
every Jew from every walk of life collides.
And for me,
this is where true peace resides.
Yes, it's noisy.
Yes, they argue.
But there's something sacred
about seeing them all together
in this space.
And I wonder:
How different will the lives of my children be from mine?
Knowing they have this— this space, this land,
this sacred ground where we all come together.
It's chaotic at times, yes.
But it's holy nonetheless.

But Now I'm Found

I WAS RAISED in the church where hearts seemed warm,
Taught that forgiveness would weather every storm.
They preached of grace, of peace so bright,
A perfect world bathed in holy light.
But beneath their verses of boundless love,
I found deceit—no truth from above.
Lies and betrayal, sharp as a knife,
Shattered my trust, uprooted my life.

Everything I'd known began to crack,
A silent truth whispered, urging me back.
I stepped beyond the painted walls,
Answering a call that echoed through the halls.

They said love endures without a break,
But once I strayed, their kindness was fake.
Cold eyes, hushed murmurs, whispers so cruel,
The crowd disappeared, leaving me the fool.
Yet each hesitant step toward ancient light
Bolstered my soul, granted me sight.
In new prayers rising, a home so strong,
I discovered I wasn't alone for long.

All that I lost returned in gold,
A love more real, a truth so bold.
The path I followed filled me with grace,
Rooted in wisdom from a sacred place.
Though they scorched me with their hatred's flame,
I carried on, unbowed by shame.

Now I see their promise was blind,
Conditioned by chains that stifled the mind.
I broke those fetters, stood tall at last,
Embraced a faith that honored my past.
Acceptance, peace—a new light dawned,
My spirit lifted, my old fears gone.

At the end of this road, I found my home,
Though all around me, the world felt alone.
In the Jewish faith, my heart found rest—
A family of truth that welcomed my quest.
And though the ones who once vowed to stay
Turned their backs and drifted away,
I am held by arms steadfast and strong,
A place where my soul has always belonged.

And Then What?

AFTERWORD

*A*s with any real life story, life continues beyond the final chapter of the book.

You've followed the highlights of my faith journey: my childhood, my deep commitment to the church and its mission, the startling discovery of truth, the challenging path to conversion, and the sense of peace and belonging I found in Torah and the Jewish community.

My aliyah and current life in Israel deserves its own book—perhaps one day I'll write it. But, because of the impact of my work today, there's an important piece I feel compelled to share now.

For my family, aliyah meant a fresh start: new friends, a new community, and the chance to be seen as just another Jewish family. It was an opportunity to leave our past behind, our blended family's story unknown, and begin anew.

Like many converts, I longed to fit in, to be seen and accepted as any other Jew. For a time, that's exactly what we did. I didn't speak of my past. My children, still young when we began this journey, knew only Jewish life. This allowed them to integrate and thrive in Israeli culture, facing challenges no different from other immigrants.

My eldest daughter attended seminary, pursued culinary school, married, and built a beautiful life here in Israel. My son completed high school, a mechina (religious preparation for military service), served in the IDF, and is now studying high-tech. I travel abroad for speaking engagements, but outside of visiting family, my children have little interest in the U.S. Israeli life, while challenging, has become their identity. Instilling a love for the land and its people in them feels like a tremendous blessing—one I could only dream of achieving.

But that fresh start? It didn't last long.

From the beginning of my Jewish journey, I was deeply involved in counter-missionary efforts. At first, it was therapeutic—a way to validate my decision and help others on similar paths. It was also a *tikkun*, a correction for the guilt I carried from leading others to Christianity. Before aliyah, my work was public, but life in Israel offered a chance to start over, so I shifted to a quieter, more private role.

That changed when I began understanding the missionary situation in Israel.

When I arrived in 2015, I researched and was shocked by what I found: 15,000 Jews identifying as "Messianic believers" and 120 Messianic congregations. These numbers were staggering. Quietly, I committed myself to working with *Jewish Israel*, an organization dedicated to exposing missionary agendas and establishing boundaries between faith-based organizations and the Israeli government.

Missionaries in Israel employ the same tactics I once used: presenting themselves as friends of Israel, focusing on love and humanitarian aid. This resonates deeply with many; but behind closed doors, they openly discuss their true mission: converting Jews to Christianity. In communications with funders, they boast about their "success," sometimes mocking Jews as gullible and celebrating how easily they can infiltrate communities by offering financial aid.

Bringing these communications to light—through videos, newsletters, or their own websites—has shocked many Israelis. Over the years, I've spoken to politicians, heads of Jewish organizations, Jewish Agency, and Knesset members. This work allowed me to make a difference while maintaining privacy about my past.

Then came 2020.

The COVID-19 pandemic changed everything. Isolation halted in-person meetings, but missionary efforts intensified. Humanitarian aid and economic despair were weaponized to target vulnerable communities. Some groups even described COVID as "God's method" to open Jewish hearts to the gospel, claiming it would trigger the second coming of Jesus.

Reevaluating my efforts, I updated the data I had compiled in 2015—and my heart sank. The numbers had doubled. By 2020, 30,000 Jews in Israel identified as Messianic believers, and there were now over 300 congregations and missionary organizations. I discovered more than 200 Israel-based websites dedicated to converting Jews, with content in Hebrew, English, and Russian.

The fight was bigger than I had imagined.

One major effort that year involved GodTV. They planned to launch a cable channel explicitly aimed at bringing the gospel into every Jewish home, boasting that this would lead to the conversion of 9 million Jews. For months, I forwarded their newsletters and videos to journalists and government officials, but no one seemed to care.

So, in quarantine, I decided to learn a new skill: video editing. I compiled clips of GodTV's bold proclamations into a single video that clearly exposed their agenda. I uploaded it to YouTube.

Overnight, the video went viral. The next day, it became a headline in *Haaretz* and then in every major news outlet across Israel. Knesset members spoke out, and the public was outraged. Within days it was worldwide news translated into every language. Jewish communities worldwide were offended, while Christian organizations cried "persecution" at the backlash.

For me, it was an opportunity to use a new medium to get my message across. News outlets began contacting me for interviews. Nervous about the exposure, I avoided using my name, though it was clearly visible on my YouTube profile. Instead, I asked that my work be attributed to "a group of concerned activists."

Thankfully, Rabbi Tovia Singer—whose work had profoundly influenced my life—had recently made aliyah before the pandemic. This gave me the chance to refer journalists to him, someone I trusted to handle public exposure with expertise.

Still, one question kept coming up: *"Who are you?"* What gave me the authority to speak about Jewish-Christian relations? What credentials qualified me to call out evangelical missionaries?

I had a decision to make.

My husband is a doctor. He has both a moral and professional obligation to answer anytime he hears the call, "Is there a doctor here?" Whether on vacation or en route to a destination, if a life is at risk, he must act.

That was the pull I felt. Reviewing the skyrocketing statistics and the GodTV case that had landed in my lap, I couldn't ignore the moral obligation to do something.

So, I began answering those questions. I knew that world because I came from it. I understood the tactics because I had employed them myself. I knew the agenda—it's ingrained in every Evangelical, beginning in childhood. After all, the movement's name says it all: *evangelize*.

This led to speaking engagements with Jewish audiences. Many told me how unique my story was, believing I must be the only person to take such a journey. But that couldn't be further from the truth. Over the past 20 years, I've met thousands—if not hundreds of thousands—of people on similar paths. While the number of Jews converting to Christianity is alarming, I'm thrilled to witness a mass exodus in the opposite direction. There's an awakening happening, and I feel privileged to see it firsthand.

In 2020, I founded Beyneynu (beyneynu.com), a 501(c)(3) non-profit organization that monitors missionary activity worldwide. We work with government and community leaders to raise awareness about the challenges while we encourage safe, consistent boundaries with faith-based organizations.

The staff and volunteers of Beyneynu are all former Christians. Like me, they bring the background and skills needed to combat this spiritual threat. Since its inception, Beyneynu has exposed numerous shocking infiltrations into Jewish communities and uncovered partnerships with seemingly "kosher" organizations that were anything but. Our work has made international headlines, disrupted missionary operations, and changed how these efforts are conducted, especially in Israel.

I never sought a career as a missionary, and knowing now the damage it caused, I'm certainly not proud of it. But it gave me the insight and skills I now use to protect my Jewish family—a family I will defend at all costs.

It's easy to point the finger at missionaries and label them as the bad guys. It's much harder to hold up a mirror and ask ourselves how we got here. In my opinion, the Jews in the church today represent the unpaid bills of the Jewish people. I know that's not an easy message to hear, but I know firsthand that missionaries intentionally target the most vulnerable and least educated.

We can do a much better job of caring for each other, healing the divisions between us, and loving every Jew, regardless of their background or religious garb. Education is key. Our young people could be inoculated from this threat if they deeply understood what it truly means to be Jewish—not just that "we don't believe in Jesus."

We should teach Tanach. Not just the nice stories, but all of it. We should know it like we know our favorite song—the one where every note and pitch change is ingrained in us. When we hear a cover of that song and even a single note is off, we recognize it immediately. If our young people knew Tanach with that same familiarity, no missionary would be able to convince them with out-of-context or mistranslated verses.

I'll continue to call out deception because the Jewish people are my family. But real change? That will have to come from all of us.

Reviews/Recommendations

"In her powerful new book, *I Once Was Lost*, Shannon Nuszen masterfully shares her unique spiritual journey through exquisite narrative poetry. Raised in an evangelical Christian home, she spent her youth passionately working to convert Jews to Christianity. Yet, in a remarkable turn of fate, Shannon's journey led her to embrace Orthodox Judaism—a transformation that not only reshaped her beliefs but also redefined her life's mission.

The profound irony of Shannon's story is striking: once committed to bringing Jews into the church, she now dedicates herself to protecting Jewish communities from the very missionaries she once stood alongside. In an astonishing twist, this pastor's daughter has helped rescue more Jews from Christianity than most rabbis!

I Once Was Lost offers a rare and deeply personal insight into her transition—from a devout fundamentalist Christian determined to convert Jews to a committed Orthodox Jew who found true spiritual liberation. This book is a testament to her extraordinary path, her unwavering faith, and her ultimate return home. Welcome home."

—Rabbi Tovia Singer, Director of Outreach Judaism and Author of "Let's Get Biblical"

"Robert Frost wrote that, 'Poetry is when an emotion has found its thought and the thought has found words.' Shannon Nuszen's stirring spiritual odyssey is beautifully related in this poetic narrative. In these moving words we meet a woman fiercely committed to truth and following G-d with passion and integrity. The poetic modality powerfully captures the deep and raw emotions experienced when the edifice of her religious life crumbled and she courageously forged ahead to build a new life. Kudos on producing this moving and inspiring autobiography."
–Rabbi Michael Skobac, Director Jews for Judaism (Canada)

"Shanon Nuszen's *I Once Was Lost* is a compelling work of narrative poetry that perfectly reflects her remarkable journey through an even more remarkable life. Her story is one of soul-searching, a quest for a genuine and consistent identity, and an inspiring path toward clarity, faith, and belonging. Trained to spread her church's message with precision and skill, Nuszen uses those very tools in this book to lay bare her innermost thoughts. She openly shares her doubts and struggles with the church while shedding light on the certainty and peace she ultimately found in Judaism.

Every Jew's connection to faith and God is deeply personal, but Shanon's journey is uniquely extraordinary—a powerful transformation shaped by her unwavering search for truth, even when it meant breaking away from convention."
–Jonathan Sacerdoti, Writer and Broadcaster

"*I Once Was Lost* is more than a memoir—it is the voice of someone who has lived through one of the most difficult and isolating experiences a person can endure and emerged with a purpose greater than herself. Shannon Nuszen didn't just walk away from a faith that once defined her—she walked toward something deeper, despite the cost. She captures the silent battles of doubt, the heartbreak of losing relationships, and the resilience it takes to stand by the truth when everything around you urges you to stay the same.

But Nuszen's journey wasn't just about personal transformation. She took the pain, the knowledge, and the experience of her past and turned it into a mission—to protect, to educate, and to safeguard Jewish souls from the very efforts she once championed. She has done what few can—taken the hardest parts of her life and used them to make the world better. This book will not just resonate; it will validate, it will awaken, and for many, it will heal. *I Once Was Lost* is not just a story—it is a testament to the power of conviction, the weight of truth, and the unshakable spirit of those who refuse to live a lie.

–Rabbi Eli Cohen, Former Director Jews for Judaism (Sydney, Australia)

"I learned so much by reading this deeply moving personal account of loss and rebirth."
–Asaf Golan, Writer

"Shannon is a powerhouse of fire and compassion. Although the work is unique itself, so is her understanding on the Missionary vs Jew conflict. Anyone honest won't feel the same in these matters after this work. "
–Nissim Black, American-Israeli rapper, songwriter, speaker, and convert to Judaism

www.ingramcontent.com/pod-product-compliance
Lightning Source LLC
Chambersburg PA
CBHW030447100526
44580CB00002B/24